Love The Earth

Illustrations by
Marty Links

Text by
Barbara Linse
and
Marilyn Knight
Text Illustrations
by
Cynthia Clark

<u>Love The Earth</u> is a tribute to two teachers
"They were the best and they were sisters,
Janet Nickelsburg and Flora Arnstein."
--Barbara Bucher Linse

This book is Literature Based with Original Poems by the Authors

About The Authors

Barbara Linse and Marilyn Knight both received B. A. and M. A. degrees
in Elementary Education, Early Childhood Education and Curriculum Develop
from San Francisco State and Stanford Universities.
Both have been classroom teachers and elementary education curriculum specialists.

Recycled Paper

Entire Contents Copyright © 1991

I S B N 1-878079-018

Art's Publications
Box 551, San Mateo, CA 94401
(415) 344-8458

Art Of Marty Links, Inc.

Printed in the United States of America

<u>The Saving Grace</u>
A Chant: Clap hands to the rhythm

It's not easy, it takes time
To help save this world of mine.
It's not easy, it takes time
To save resources from decline.
It's not easy, it takes time,
To rid the beach of trash and slime.
It's not easy, but let's try
To <u>*Love The Earth*</u> and clean the sky.

---by Barbara Linse

Love the Earth.
It's the Planet of Our Birth.

You know, if we trash our earth, we don't get a new one. It's not like when you go to the store and get a new pair of shoes and in 3 months or so, you wear them out and then you go back to the store and get a new pair of shoes. But if we trash our earth we don't get a new one 'cause we can't just go to the store and get a new earth. We have to keep the one we have. So if we only have one earth, we had better take good care of it.

Elyce Petker, Age 9

Introduction

Man is said to be the only animal capable of changing the environment. If this statement is viewed from an historical perspective the impact of technological discoveries on the planet earth is staggering. More important however, may be the effect of the changing world on values and attitudes. How much different the advice to "eat it up, wear it out, do without" of the depression years and the admonition "a penny saved is a penny earned" to the recent "use it a day, then throw it away" and the enticing "fly now--pay later".

The concern for the environment has grown as the evidence mounts to indicate how much is in jeopardy.

This book is dedicated to the premise that the sooner awareness begins and positive habit patterns are formed, the better! Young children will be influenced by the significant adults in their lives. Parents and teachers have the opportunity to help change the world with children side by side.

-- Marilyn Knight

Table of Contents

In Each Chapter There Are:

1. *Rhymes and Reasons*
2. *Class Acts* (Science)
3. *Be Art Smart* (Art Activities)

ENJOY FRESH AIR!

What is it?

SOME FACTS

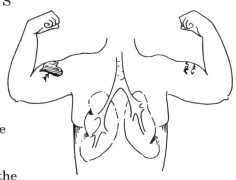

We breathe air for the oxygen we need to keep us alive. Oxygen is in the air. We have lungs and every time we breathe in air, it goes through our nose or mouth to our lungs, into our blood streams, and all through our bodies. That is where it needs to be. We breathe out carbon dioxide that plants need for survival.

Growing plants make oxygen to purify the air for us.

POEM
Where's The Air?
(With some adjusting, sing to tune "LondonBridge")

There is air around us all.
   It lives inside a bouncing ball.
We trap it in a fat balloon.
   It sits right on a little spoon.

All growing plants make oxygen
   That's in the air we breathe and then,
When air is dirty, there's pollution.
   We must find a clean solution.

A CLASS ACT: <u>Does air have weight?</u>

Materials: 2 balloons, a stick and some string.

Let's do it:

Tie the string in the middle of a stick. Someone may hold the stick by the string. Blow up balloons to the same size and fasten a string around tops. Tie a balloon on each end of the stick. Pop one balloon and whoops, the fat balloon is heavier, just look. Pop the second balloon and the stick is level again.

What happened?
Full balloons are heavier than popped balloons.
So air must have weight.

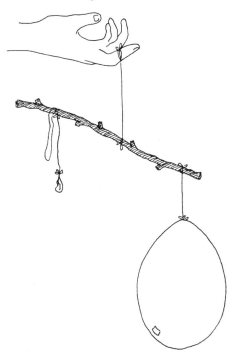

1

A CLASS ACT: <u>Air Pollution Detectives</u>

Materials: A coffee filter and a funnel for each child.

Discuss places where air may get dirty or stay cleaner. Allow each youngster to become a pollution detective by placing a filter in the funnel.

Let's see what happens!

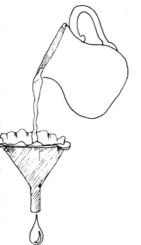

Youngsters will put their "pollution detective equipment" in a special spot such as on a window ledge, in a garage at home, on their desks, etc. Label each with child's name. Leave in place for several days.

Have youngsters examine their "detective equipment" for differences. Look at dry filters. Pour water through them. What happened?

A CLASS ACT: <u>Is It Polite To Pollute?</u>

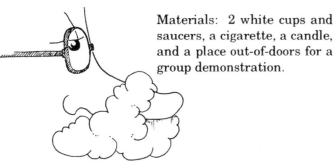

Materials: 2 white cups and saucers, a cigarette, a candle, and a place out-of-doors for a group demonstration.

Here's what to do:

Light candle and cigarette. Hold over saucer. Place cups over candle and cigarette. Remove cup, repeating the process <u>until cup or saucer looks smokey</u>.

Question: What was made? **Pollution**. What if a whole roomful of people were smoking or were careless with candles?

BE ART SMART: <u>A Rosey Posey Potpourri</u>

Materials: A recycled container such as a cottage cheese carton or styrofoam tray, some flower petals (roses smell sweetest), salt, orange peel cut up, crushed cloves, an old sheet cut into squares 12" x 12" (one for each child), some ribbon, yarn or string, poster paint, a brush, and 1 tablespoon of kitchen cleanser per cup of paint.

Let's Make it!

Paint carton, let dry between colors.

Place sheet square in container, centered. Put some petals, orange peel, and cloves on the square. Sprinkle salt lightly over mixture. Make several layers. Place in a dark, airy place for 10 days.

Remove from hiding place and sniff it. Gather sheeting by corners. Tie with a string or ribbon. Put back in its pretty container for children to take home for sweeter, fresher air.

QUESTIONS:

What lovely gift does a growing plant give us? (Answer: **Oxygen**!)

What can we use up with too many people and smoke and flames? (Answer: **Oxygen**!)

USE RECYCLED PAPER!

FACT

Most paper is made from trees. If we get in the habit of reusing paper products and using paper on both sides, we will help protect and save our forests. These habits of conservation are easiest to learn when we are very young.

POEM

Fold paper bags straight from the store.
Use them 3 times, 6 times, more.
Plastic bags take too much space.
Forever on our earth! Disgrace!

BE ART SMART: Beautiful Old Bags

Materials: Old shopping bags, markers or crayons.

Let's make it!

Children dress up old bags for home shopping with "To Market to Market to Buy a Fat Pig" or their own words. Children might make drawing on the sides.

BE ART SMART: Make Mr. Greene Paperony?

Materials: Grass seeds, used paper cups, planter mix, and magic markers.

Let's make it!

Each little gardener will make a face on a cup with markers. Put planter mix in the cup, plant seeds and soon you'll have a surprise.

BE ART SMART: Sunday Funnies Waste Basket

Materials: A stack of newspapers including Sunday funnies, paste thinned with water, paper clips, a piece of corrugated cardboard.

Here's how you make it:

On a washable surface, lay whole sheets of newspaper, spreading each surface with paste until you have 6 layers. Make seventh layer with colored comics. While still damp, roll unto a cylinder. Smear one edge with unthinned paste and lap over opposite edge, making a straight seam.

Secure top and bottom with paper clips. Allow to dry until stiff. Cut a circle from corrugated cardboard to fit bottom of cylinder. Fasten to cylinder with masking tape. Conceal with pasted strips of funnies. Let dry for 3 or 4 days. Paint with canned milk to make it glossy.

BE ART SMART: Make Wrapping Paper

Materials You'll Need: Big grocery bags cut open, poster paint, brushes, easy to find printers such as potato mashers, jar lids, shells, cookie cutters, pebbles, forks. Newspapers and rags for practice prints and cleanup.

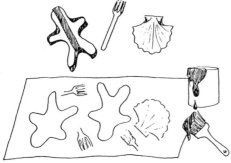

Here's how you do it!

Apply paint to printer with a wide brush. Press printer on prepared bags. Use one design and one color at a time. Let dry between applications. These make lovely wall hangings or they can wrap gifts nicely.

BE ART SMART: Baggy Puppetry

Materials: Used lunch bags, construction paper, paste, and scissors.

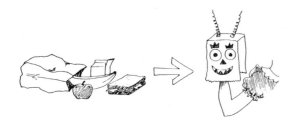

The drawing shows best how this valuable craft is put together. Children can be as creative with these hand puppets as the imagination will allow. Encourage them to add yarn, buttons, artificial flowers, artificial fruit, cotton.

When you see this symbol it means the paper used is recycled. _Love the Earth_ is printed on recycled paper.

A CLASS ACT: Make Your Own Paper

Materials: Fine grasses and cotton lint, paper toweling, facial tissue, large tub of water, a bit of white glue, pieces of wire screen the size of paper you wish to make. Optional, but a good tool if you can find one, is an old blender (and it will get messy).

This is almost magic. Try it!

You put cotton lint and grasses in a tub of water into which you have placed a bit of white glue. The ingredients are mixed thoroughly so that all particles are floating freely in the water bath. To help break down fibers, an old blender is most convenient for the finer the bits of grass, lint, or paper particles, the finer the paper you will be able to make.

Take the piece of wire screen and place it flat on the bottom of tub of water. Bring screen directly out of the water holding it parallel with bottom of tub, catching pieces of the grass, lint, and paper. The thin coating of fibers in the water will become your home-made paper after it is allowed to dry.

To hurry the drying process, place screen and lint or grass particles that were collected, on a flat surface, perhaps on a towel which will absorb some of the moisture. As soon as possible, remove screen and leave newly made paper on the towel to firm up. After it has dried for perhaps a day, you can make surface of the paper smoother by using a warm iron.

BE ART SMART: Treasure Holders

Materials: Used manila envelopes, construction paper and magic markers.

Merely pretty-up large used envelopes for keepsake storage places. Addressed side of envelope can be covered with paper designs that hide all.

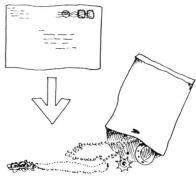

EAT NUTRITIOUSLY!

FACT

Good eating habits have to be formed when we are young. Problems such as anorexia, obesity, or sloppy nutrition may be best counteracted by knowing what good nutrition is, making the facts about nutrition available, and arranging for eating to be fun. Perhaps there are ideas here you may wish to copy for your youngsters to take home.

POEM
Incredible Edibles
(Sing to tune of "Baa Baa Black Sheep")

Meat and vegies, fruit and fish,
Have some chicken if you wish.
Bread and butter, eggs and cheese,
Chew your food and please say "please".
We will eat nutritiously,
Good for you, and good for me!

Eat something from each of these food groups every day if you can.

A CLASS ACT: Be A Milk Tester

Materials: 3 clear glasses, samples of whole milk, slim milk, heavy cream, an eye dropper.

To do it:

One at a time, collect a drop from one of the milk samples and drop it into a clean glass. Do a different milk sample into another glass and compare the difference of how the drops came out of the dropper. (The creamiest is the thickest and the heaviest while the slim milk is the lightest and moves more quickly through the dropper.) You might compare how each sample tastes.

A CLASS ACT: Hallowinners

Materials: Pumpkins, gourds, winter squash, food coloring, kitchen cleanser, a paint brush for each color, and a container for each color.

To do it:

Paint pumpkin or squash with a solution of 1 cup water and 1 tablespoon kitchen cleanser.

Let dry. Using food colors, paint on a wonderful face, color by color. (You can mix colors in advance in a separate container.).

Use your Winner as a decoration for a couple of weeks. After Halloween, wash pumpkin thoroughly, cut it open, take out seeds, cut up pumpkin and cook it for dinner.

Put 2-5 cups water in a sauce pan. Add pumpkin and salt. Cook until tender. Drain off water, add butter or margerine. Enjoy!

Wash, dry, and bake seeds on a cookie sheet for 30 minutes in a 225 degree oven.

A CLASS ACT: <u>Make Yogurt Cheese</u>
(Something delicious and good for you, too.)

Materials: 2 to 3 cups regular plain yogurt, 1 package softened cream cheese (optional), fresh herbs such as basil, garlic, chives, oregano, or perhaps olives. You will also need a cheese cloth or dampened coffee filter, a small colander (preferably stainless steel or plastic), a large bowl, rubber spatula, knife and cutting board.

And this is all you do!

Put cheese cloth or coffee filter into colander and place in a big bowl. Spoon yogurt into colander and let sit at least 12 hours to drain. It is all right for it to sit up to 24 hours, for the longer it sits, the more dense it becomes. Once drained, put in a clean bowl, add cream cheese, and blend well. It is optional to mince herbs and blend into cheese. Make shapes (logs or balls) out of the cheese and serve with crackers at snack time.

Hint: Use whole plain yogurt for low-fat does not yield much. Regrigerate after blending cheese and herbs. This makes it easier to form into shapes.

A CLASS ACT: <u>Grow Some Vegetables</u>

Materials: A little piece of earth. Size can vary from a planter box to a garden plot. If a planter box is used, you will need some planter mix, packages of carrots, parsley, and radish seeds.

To do it:

Following directions on seed packages. Let each youngster plant some seeds, help care for the growing plants, harvest vegetables and share them for good eating.

A CLASS ACT: <u>Color of Onions</u>

Materials: Yellow onions or red onions, or both. A pan, water, a stove, a piece of clean white cloth at least 12" x 12", a bit of salt.

Here's how:

Take outer peeling of an onion (keep colors separate) and put in the pan. Add a pinch of salt. Put at least 1 cup of water in the pan and bring to a boil. Let simmer for 5 minutes. Allow liquid to cool and dip clean cloth into liquid. Soak for at least an hour. Try it again with a different color of onion peel. This is a truly safe vegetable dye.

(HINT: Red onion skins make gorgeous colored hard cooked eggs at holiday time.)

BE ART SMART: <u>Good Eating Collages</u>

Materials: Background paper such as butcher paper, shelf paper or newsprint, paste, scissors, pictures of good healthful food. These may be drawn by the children or cut from recycled magazines.

Collages may be made by each child or made together by the whole group.

Getting it together:

Gather pictures together and sort them according to food groups, foods for breakfast, lunch or dinner, or types of meals such as salads, school lunches, after school snacks.

You might suggest motivating titles as "Meet Vita Minnie", "Grow up with healthful food" or "Dinner for a Giant." Some girls and boys may arrange their's to make pleasing patterns and designs on the background paper. Paste them in place on the paper and display these for pleasure and for good ideas.

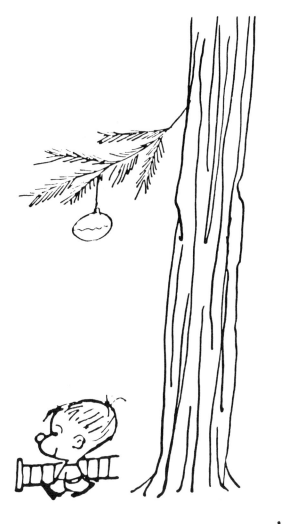

SAVE OUR TREES !

FACT

Trees make our world a better place by providing oxygen, shelter for animals, food to eat, and are a source of materials to make wooden buildings, paper, and other products. These are our special gifts from trees.

HOME SWEET HOME

POEM

What's In A Tree?
(With GREAT imagination you may be able to fit these words to the tune "London Bridge")

Children may put arms in a circle to show "around a tree" when they say sycamore, maple, hickory and apple tree. Arms go straight up for evergreens such as hemlock and redwoods.

There's no sweet sap in a sycamore tree,
Sycamore tree, sycamore tree.
There's no sweet sap in a hemlock tree,
No sweet sap.

But sweet sap comes from the sugar maple tree,
Sugar maple tree, sugar maple tree.
And it's as sweet as it can be,
Sweet as it can be.

There are no needles on a hickory tree,
Hickory tree, hickory tree.
There are no needles on an apple tree,
None on an apple tree.

But needles come from an evergreen tree,
Evergreen tree, evergreen tree.
And they're as sharp as sharp can be,
As sharp as they can be.

Would you like to be an evergreen tree,
Or lose your leaves and feel free?
But then you'd be a deciduous tree,
With branches for all to see.

Are ice cream cones in a redwood tree?
No, that's as silly as silly can be.
A redwood is a conifer tree.
There are cones in a redwood tree.

A CLASS ACT: <u>Rubbadub Trees</u>

POEM
<u>What's That In Your Tub?</u>

It's bark as you see,
And leaves from a tree.
With paper and crayons
Have a rubadub spree.

Materials: Leaves, pine needles, tree bark, newsprint or tissue paper.

Here's how you do it:

Arrange leaves and needles on a stack of newspapers. Place a sheet of newsprint on tissue paper over them. With peeled crayons, using the broad side, rub over surface, one color at a time.

Do trees help us stay clean?

A REAL CLASSY ACT: <u>Quick Leaf Notes</u>

Materials: Leaves (green or colored), liquid starch, a brush, scissors, waxed paper, white tissue, and a short stack of newspapers on which children will work.

Let's make the leaf notes:

Put down a sheet of waxed paper 6" x 6" or larger and spread starch over it. For a bright spot on finished work, arrange a small cluster of leaves at top of paper, at the bottom, or at a corner. Cover with white tissue. Remove from "short stack" to keep it from sticking.

BE ART SMART: <u>Rings for Cloth Napkins</u>

These are nice gifts to take home and you don't have to cut down trees as you do when you use paper napkins.

Materials: Cardboard tubes from paper rolls (waxed paper, toilet tissue, or paper towels). You will also need liquid starch, yarn, colored tissue paper, scissors, and masking tape.

Here is all you do:

Tape waxed paper on desk or table to keep things clean.

Cut tubes into 2" lengths. Tear strips or squares of colored tissue, dip into starch, squeeze off excess liquid and press onto cardboard tubes. It's fun to change colors. Encourage children to press yarn patterns onto tubes.

SAVE WATER!

FACT

Water covers about 70% of the surface of the earth. All living things are made up largely of water. Water is also in air, oceans, earth, rivers and ponds. Water cycle is continuous. Heat from the sun evaporates water from the earth and transforms it into clouds. Cooling brings precipitation in the form of rain or snow. Rain or snow water percolates into the earth or the rivers, seas, or lakes and it is ready to be used by living creatures.

POEM

Water Water Everywhere, (After a good rain)
If you work at it, you can sing it to the tune "Mary Had A Little Lamb".

Water helps the trees to grow,
Trees to grow, trees to grow.
It comes from rain and melting snow,
Hey now, its good to drink.

We use it daily when we shower,
When we shower, when we shower.
And cook, and drink, and water flowers,
Hey now, we really need it.

We mustn't waste a single drop,
A single drop, a single drop.
Because our short supply could stop.
Hey now, we can't have that.

Now, when you sing this little song,
This little song, this little song,
Then save a drop, you can't go wrong.
Hey now, we need it so!

A REAL CLASS ACT: When you Brush Your Teeth

Materials: A bowl in the sink, tooth brush, tooth paste, a measuring cup.

Let's all try this at home:

Put bowl in the sink and brush your teeth the regular way. When you are finished use the measuring cup to measure amount of water in the bowl.

Now, Brush to Save Water:

Wet toothbrush, put paste on brush, then brush teeth. Use more water only for rinsing. Which way saves the most water?

Other Saving Ways:

Catch rainwater in a bucket to water plants in the house and garden.

Take short showers.

Save water when you wash clothes and use it to bathe the dog or water the garden.

Can you think of other Saving Ways?

A CLASS ACT: <u>Which Weighs More, Water or Ice?</u>

Materials: Food coloring, water, a cup, a bowl, a fridge.

Let's find the answer.

Ice is frozen water. Put some food coloring in a bowl of water. Pour into an ice cube tray. Freeze. Pour a cup of clear water into bowl and add colored ice cubes. Watch the frozen water float on top. Ice is lighter than water.

Fill a waxed milk carton half full of water. Mark water line. Freeze it. Where is the water line, now? In freezing weather, what part of a pond is ice? The top, because ice is lightest.

How do people fish in a frozen lake? They dig a little hole in the ice.

A CLASS ACT: <u>Who Stole the Water?</u>

Materials: 2 jars the same size, marking pen or masking tape, foil.

Let's see:

Fill jars with water. Cover one tightly with foil. Leave the other one open.

Put both jars in a warm place for 5 days. Now, check water levels and mark those levels on the outside of jars. Use pen or tape.

What happened to the water levels and why do you think it did?

(A secret to the teacher: Water level on the open jar should be the lowest. Water escaped into the air as vapor or moist air. Foil kept water in the covered jar. This process is <u>evaporation</u>.)

BE ART SMART: <u>Pretty Paper Washes</u>

Materials: Most any kind of paper from tissue paper to newsprint, watercolors, washable markers, brushes, a container of rain water or salty sea water.

Let's Do It:

Wet paper well and make color puddles with paint or markers. With straw, lift water from container and blow it into color puddle on the paper. Let portions dry and make new color puddles, repeating the process. Let dry and hang up on a wire or bulletin board to brighten a spot.

Talk about the clean look water gives.

WARNING: Never, never play with water when blowing. You'll be a water waster.

KEEP OUR WORLD SAFE!

FACT

A Key word: <u>Biodegradable</u> - Means substances which can decompose and again become part of the earth. This includes natural materials as opposed to plastics, for example, which are unsafe for our fragile earth.

POEM
<u>What Is Biodegradable?</u>

Bio-degradable what is that?
Is it a plastic, or a paper hat?
A banana peeling, or a ping pong ball?
A styrofoam tray or a tree that's tall.

Cups, packing materials, fast food trays and other styrofoam pests just do not decompose. They stay in the earth forever.

POEM
<u>Banish Styrofoam</u>
(Sing to "Baa, Baa, Black Sheep")

Keep styrofoam from land to gutter
It just makes a whole lot of clutter.
Don't even bring it to your home
Let's never make more styrofoam.
It will never decompose,
Where will it go, do you suppose?

A balloon that's inflatable's not biodegradable.

Never let go of helium-filled balloons out of doors. In the ocean they sometimes look like such creatures as jelly fish and are eaten by animals which then may choke to death.

IT'S NOT A CLASS ACT: An Oil Spill

Materials: 2 large glass jars containing water, salad oil, 2 or 3 bath towels, bird feathers, bits of fur.

Let's see what happens:

Pour 1/4 cup salad oil into one jar. Add fur and feathers.

Take out fur and feathers. Put them on towels. What is the difference? What happens to sea and air creatures when oil gets into their waters?

Until we can replace styrofoam meat trays, we may as well recycle them.

A CLASS ACT: Biodegradable, Positive Proof

Materials: 1/2 gallon milk cartons, soil, scissors, tape. Any number of things such as an apple core, a wooden match, a green leaf, some metal foil, a candy wrapper, a short piece of string, a plastic container top, a soda bottle top.

Let's do it!

Place many of these items in a milk carton and cover with soil, making sure all items are beneath the soil. Put containers in a rather warm place. Each week empty out boxes, one at a time, on newspapers. Discuss what each item looks like. Keep track of your findings each week, perhaps on a chart. After 8 weeks remove contents and separate. Which objects were biodegradable?

Girls and boys draw pictures of their favorite things that have gotten rotten.

BE ART SMART: Marble Magic From Oil
                                    and Water

Materials: White drawing paper or manila paper, newsprint or recycled newspapers, scissors, colored chalk, model airplane paint, salad oil, a sink or pan to hold water and a sheet of paper.

Let's make it beautiful:

Fill container half full of water. Scrape chalk shavings and add oil or float model airplane paint on the water. Swirl around. See how separate the oil is from the water. Pull a piece of paper through the water.

Hang the paper to dry and look pretty. Oil, chalk, paint and water make beautiful patterns on paper, but oil and water make a terrible, deadly mess in the ocean.

BE KIND TO ANIMALS!

FACT

Humans can make it easy or hard for animals to exist. We are the only animals who can change the environment to suit their needs. They become unable to live in their changed world and so become extinct. *Extinct* means that there are no more of a particular animal. *Endangered* means a particular animal is in danger of becoming extinct. Among those endangered animals that could become extinct are African elephants that are killed regularly for their ivory tusks, and beavers, red foxes, lynx and wolves which are killed for their furs.

POEM
Animals
(May be sung to tune "Farmer In the Dell")

Some monkeys sleep in trees,
And penguins never freeze.
An elephant can weigh two tons,
And skunks don't seem to please.

(Have class make up verses.)

A CLASS ACT: Adopt An Animal

Your class or friends can adopt an animal to make sure it gets the protection it needs.

To learn more write to:
American Association of Zoological
Parks and Aquariums
4550 Montgomery Avenue, Suite 940
N. Bethessda, MD 20814

An animal thing to do: Go visit your local zoo

Visit zoos and see before your eye how many groups of animals are protected from extinction. Some zoos have special environments, such as rain forests for tigers and caves for gorillas.

Nature has made wonderful provisions for animals. The polar bear was given a thick white coat to be invisible and warm in the white frozen north. Sometimes we cause problems for animals. We destroy their homes when we cut down trees and take the wood to build houses for people.

For *lists of endangered species*, write:

Office of Endangered
Species
Fish and Wildlife
Service
U. S. Department of the
Interior
Washington, DC 20240

U. S. Environmental
Protection Agency
401 M. Street, SW A106
Washington, DC 20460

Way to go!

SOME VERY CLASSY ACTS:

Write to and visit Wild Life Sanctuaries where needy animals such as squirrels and other woodland creatures might have a broken leg mended.

Write to and visit The Humane Society nearest you. You can see, and even adopt, animals, usually pets, who need good homes.

Visit a farm or circus to see animals that work for a living. Are they well cared for? Record animal sounds round about you.

Have a pet parade at school. Be sure to plan this well in advance. Make a video of the event.

Be sure you do not use poisonous pest killers at home where there are pets and people. Brewer's yeast, cream of tarter and dried pepper are pet-safe deterrents.

They'll only shoo a flea,
They won't hurt you or me.

EVERYBODY HELP:

Fill your room with books, pictures, and videos about animals. Find tapes of animal voices.
Perhaps you can give a home to a rabbit, a hamster or a fish.

Share pictures of animals that have special behaviors or needs. Share questions as:
Why do monkeys like trees?
What kind of roof does a giraffe need and why?

Pets, Pets, Pets

We love our dogs,
We love our cats.
Our birds and rabbits, too.
I wouldn't want to do a thing,
To harm a pet, would you?

Tattle Tails

A happy dog wags its tail
A furious cat wags its tail
A frightened dog puts its tail between its legs.
A happy cat puts his tail between its legs.

BE ART SMART: Let's Make Animal Faces

Materials: Paper plates, paste, crayons, markers, scissors, scrap of cloth, yarn, string and other recyclables.

To do it:

Open the possibilities: brown yarn is monkey fur, fringed paper is a lion's mane. What else do your recyclables want to become? Turn plates into animal faces to hang around the room, wear in a zoo play or to a Halloween party. String or yarn stapled on can hold the face in place.

BE AN ORGANIC GARDENER!

We'll focus on the cultivation of growing things while working with nature. The relationship between plants, animals and their environments is essential. We'll explore ways to grow by using natural fertilizers and deterrents to insects in our gardens rather than chemical pesticides.

POEM
The Organic Gardener
(Can be sung to tune of "Farmer in the Dell")

Be an organic gardener
With nature as your partner
Let lady bugs nibble your insects for you
Make chemicals strictly taboo. *(Children shake their fingers).*

Word: Taboo = something you must not do.

SOME REAL CLASSY ACTS:

Some natural ways to get rid of insects:
1. Brush both sides of growing leaves with flour.
2. Sprinkle salt between rows of growing plants.
3. Scatter garlic cloves in the garden.

Some natural ways to clean:
Get rid of aerosol cans!
1. Use inside of a banana peel to polish shoes.
2. Polish silver with toothpaste.
3. Dip a cotton ball in vanilla to set on a table or in the fridge. Oh, does it smell nice!

Make a Snail Trail or Slug It Out, A Surprise:

You'll Need: A snail or a slug, some black paper and adult helpers.

Lay "pests" on paper. Nudge them gently with a little stick to get them to crawl and watch them make a silver trail. This is mucous. Doesn't it look pretty?

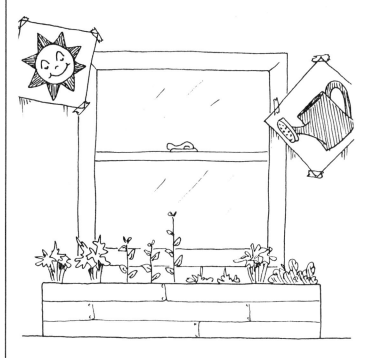

15

A CLASS ACT: <u>Very Natural Fertilizer</u>
(This is as classy as it gets!)

(Let's make it at least 3' x 4')
Construct a box with loose-fitting boards or perhaps place some chicken wire around secure corners such as posts driven into the ground.

It may be a good idea to leave an opening at the bottom of the "container" so that ready-to-use compost can be scraped out easily.

What to put in the compost pile:
Autumn leaves, grass clippings, twigs, eggshells, vegetable peelings or anything biodegradable from the kitchen or the yard.

The Compost Chant

Cobs from corn,
Unused meat.
Apple cores,
Cake that's sweet.
Put these in your compost pile,
Make your garden grow in style.

Be sure you make a tall heap. Cover with an old rug, a sheet, or newspapers. Wet it down in the fall. It will decompose in the winter. By spring you will have fine organic fertilizer to make your garden grow.

A CLASS ACT: <u>Bottle Garden</u>

Materials: Wide mouth jars, sand, charcoal, pebbles, ferns, mosses, and if possible, tiny branches covered with lichen.

Spoon pebbles into bottom of jar. Add a layer of charcoal. Next, add a 3-inch layer of soil and press down. Dig a hole in soil for each plant and press firmly into the earth. Be sure roots are well covered. Moss needs gentle treatment but will grow on soil. This is a garden and needs to be watered, fed, and pruned as does any other garden.

BE ART SMART: <u>Sammy Scarecrow</u>

Materials: Lots of old, runny panty hose, string, long sleeved shirts, pants, dresses, an old broomstick or a long stick (perhaps even 2 sticks), some yarn, hat and gloves.

To do it:

Use longest broom stick you can find as the base. Tie a panty-hose-stuffed dress or shirt and pants around the pole. Stuff more panty hose with other panty hose for legs, feet, arms, hands, and a head tied at the top. You might add yarn hair and a hat. Put it in the garden and watch what happens.

16

PicK up TRASH !

FACT

Trash on the earth is killing our animals, for sometimes they eat it and it is not digestible. A particular danger is that plastics even get into our oceans and animals of the sea eat them.

Also, trash does not look good and makes the earth have a cluttered appearance. Because of all of these facts, many of our states are so concerned about trash along the roadsides that people are fined if they drop litter.

POEM
TheTrashy Blues
("Itsy Bitsy Spider" fits this poem quite well)

A little bit of garbage
Fell into a pail. Kerplop!
With papers, cans'n bottles,
It didn't seem to stop.
It reached up to the ceiling,
It almost touched the wall
And to see above
 th' garbage,
You had to be quite tall.

So mom said, "Hey, look kids,
There's got to be a way.
To get rid of all the garbage,
Good! Jenny saved the day.
Come on folks, let's recycle
Our papers, bottles, cans.
Look up in your directory
And call the recycling man.

Bash Trash and Let's Do It!

Pick up any trash you see even if it is not yours. Be sure there are trash cans in your home. Look for trash cans in public places and use them!

A CLASS ACT: Love Letters

Here are some names of "Trash Experts." You may wish to write letters with children to get "Trash Ideas" for your class to learn more about the problem.

Defenders of Wildlife
1244 19th Street NW
Washington, DC 20036
Request the booklet entitled, *Deadly Throwaways*.

The Center for Marine Conservation
1725 DeSales St. NW, Suite 500
Washington, DC 20036
Ask for information on cleaning up our beaches.

Recycling is using materials over and over-again.

Have labeled containers for everything. Use picture labels for young children. Explain that glass will be melted into new glass. Aluminum cans, foil, frozen dinner holders will be melted into aluminum bars and used again. Newspapers can be processed to be used again.

Recycle toys or clothes by passing them on to another child when you are through with them.

The Awful Truth is that nature is in trouble because of the litter we leave behind.

1. Many animals have been cut on half-opened soda cans.
2. Others have gotten sick from eating our trash such as plastic lids, styrofoam objects and food wrappers.
3. Beach and ocean litter is a special problem since sand is soft and our litter sinks into it easily. In water, some plastic looks like jelly fish and is eaten. It can kill. Forgotten fishing lines can tangle and injure sea creatures.

A CLASS ACT: Beachcombing

Materials: A collection plate which could be a "recycled" paper plate or paper bag and perhaps a mache egg carton for saveables.

Here's how:

Collect treasures from the beach -little pieces of driftwood, special stones and shells. Be sure they will fit into egg carton sections. Adults can help youngsters identify and label each treasure.

ALMOST MORE IMPORTANT
Be sure to have an extra bag for litter you find along the way. Comb the beach with the intention of being RID of the LITTER.

YES, PICK UP TRASH !

A CLASS ACT: Let's Make Waves

Materials: Bottle with screw lid, white vinegar, salad oil, blue, red, and green food coloring.

Here's how:

Fill a bottle one third full with salad oil. Add a few drops of green and blue food coloring. Fill bottle with vinegar. Gently roll the bottle for an ocean experience. Add red food coloring and you'll really change the appearance of your ocean.

A horrible surprise! Can you make a beautiful ocean look polluted? What color did you use?

> Little drops of water,
> Little grains of sand,
> Make the beauteous ocean
> And the mighty land.
> --Robert Louis Stevenson

BE ART SMART: Sand Painting

Materials: Beach sand, food coloring, sheets of heavy cardboard (from recycling box), white glue, recycled quart jars (one for each color you plan to use), a pencil or marker, newspapers.

Let's make it.

Using the quart jars, put one-half cup water in each. Add 10 or more drops of food coloring into each jar. Red, blue, yellow and green are basic colors. To make other colors, use:
Violet = 5 drops of red and 5 drops of blue
Orange = 5 drops of red and 5 drops of yellow.

After you have water and a different food color in each jar, add enough beach sand to fill jars about half full. Shake jars to distribute color throughout the sand.

On heavy cardboard (the heavier the better to keep warping at a minimum) draw a simple picture or design. Use a colored marker to show sand color for each section. Spread glue on one colored section at a time. Then pour a colored sand on that glued section. Pour off excess sand and return it to the proper jar.

Continue, one color at a time, being sure to use enough glue to make the colored sand stick well.

The Navajo Indians in Arizona make beautiful sand paintings from their desert sand. They love the earth the same as we do!

BEFRIEND BiRDS !

FACT

Learn about endangered birds. Birds need food all year round, especially in winter. Some birds will actually feed on flowers. Their favorites are honeysuckle, rambling roses, bittersweet, buckthorn and flowering cherries. Most birds feed on insects or caterpillars that live in flowers.

The homing pigeon is a bird that can find its home and carry messages to it. All birds have homes in which they live and raise their young. Some change their address often.

POEM
A Homing We Will Go

Birds are almost everywhere
Their nests are quite amazing.
And often after moving in
Young birdies they'll be raising.

SOME CLASS ACTS: Easy Feeders

(Materials and processes listed together)

1. Merry Christmas! String popcorn with cranberries, raisins, peanuts, and popcorn.

2. String unshelled peanuts as "hang ups".

3. Nature's Way. Save pumpkin seeds, sunflower seeds, and other natural goodies. Mix these with birdseed and put them in bird feeders.

ANOTHER CLASS ACT: Make Fatsickles for the Winter Wonderland

Materials: Pieces of fat from meat, twigs 2 or 3 inches long, an ice cube tray and a freezer.

Here is how we do it:

Put fat into ice cube trays. Stick a twig in middle of each piece of fat. (The twig is the handle). Freeze. The fat stays fresh and the "sickles" are easy to pop on a branch, a pinecone, or a fence.

19

Did you know? The bald eagle and the dodo bird are close to extinction. They are endangered because of problem people who cut down trees or start fires with careless matches that make our fine feathered friends lose their homes.

SOME CLASSY ACTS: <u>Let's Go House Hunting</u>

You'll want to learn more about birds and help them a little.
1. Look for bird's nests but don't move them.
2. You might put nesting materials out in the open, such as yarn, string, thread, small strips of cloth, empty onion or orange mesh sacks. See if the birds take them away.
4. Challenge: Can you make a bird's nest? Try it.

<u>The Dirty Birds.</u>

Let's clean them up:

You'll need: Garbage can lids, old roasters or old pie pans which can become bird baths or skating rinks in winter.

Putting water in these containers makes a bird bath. Try to put them near a tree so the birds can dry their feathers on the leaves or just be able to sit at a safe place and flutter a bit.

Let's Share: At sharing time at school, encourage children to share feathers, photos, magazine pictures of birds, abandoned bird nests, labeled bird eggs, tapes of bird songs, and maybe a pet bird.

Here's a thought: Turn toilet paper rolls or other cylinders into make-believe field glasses to watch the birds. That's real recycling.

from <u>Nest of Eggs</u>
by Robert Louis Stevenson

BIRDS all the sunny day
  Flutter and quarrel
Here in the arbour-like
  Tent of the laurel.

Here in the fork
  The brown nest is seated;
Four little blue eggs
  The mother keeps heated.

While we stand watching her,
  Staring like gabies,
Safe in each egg are the
  Bird's little babies.

Soon the frail eggs they shall
  Chip, and upspringing
Make all the April woods
  Merry with singing.

A CLASS ACT: <u>Eggcentricities</u>

Teachers, parents: Work with youngsters as they poke a hole in each end of an egg. Blow contents into recycled cup.

Ready, Get Set, -----Blow!

Rinse out egg shell with cool water. Save contents in fridge for making scrambled eggs.

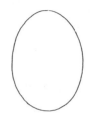

A CLASS ACT: <u>Elegant Eggs</u>

Materials: Empty egg shells, white glue, torn colored sheets from magazines, cloth and clear nail polish.

Cover egg shell with glue. Press pieces of cloth or paper onto gooey, gluey shell in a pretty pattern. Let dry. Cover egg with 2 coats of clear nail polish.

BE ART SMART: <u>A Tisket, A Tasket</u>

The original spring basket was a bird's nest. The phoney grass used in them symbolizes nesting materials used by birds.

Materials: Newspapers, big scissors, your favorite May basket pattern and material to make it, crayons and markers for decorating baskets. Decorate and assemble baskets for holding the "Elegant Egg Shells."

CONSERVE ENERGY!

FACT

Conservation does not come automatically when we are born. It is important to learn early how to conserve energy, and as children grow, to learn why we must do it.

POEM
Does Sol Perplex Us?
(Sol=Sun)

Energy comes from the sun
It keeps you warm,
And you'll have fun
Enjoying ultra-violet rays
Some sunburns last
For days and days
Wear a hat and
Sunscreen, too.
Direct sun's too much for you,
Especially in Timbuktoo
Gather rays for use in homes
In sun collectors shaped like domes.
Even water from the sea
Gives energy to you and me
Or rushing water from a river
That's oh, so cold it makes you shiver.
A windmill gives us energy
With flying arms for all to see
For heat and light most every hour
Yes, energy will give us power.
But let's be careful how we use it.
Don't use too much or we might lose it.

Let children draw pictures of their favorite part of this poem.

A CLASS ACT: Gathering Heat

Materials: Pie tins, black paint, white paint.

Let's do it!

Paint one tin white and the other black. Put them in the sun for half an hour. Feel them. Which one is warmest?

A CLASS ACT: Hot Juice

Materials: Grape juice, apple juice, 2 recycled styrofoam cups, a thermometer.

What's next?

Pour grape juice in one cup and apple juice in the other. Leave them in the sun for 2 hours. Take their temperatures. Which is warmest?

Dark colors absorb heat more readily than light colors. Now, let's drink the" hot juice".

Guess What? Clothing has seasons. In winter, clothes are often darkest and absorb heat. In summer, they are lightest in color to keep us cooler.

21

A little homework for everyone:

1. Wear sweaters in the house if you are chilly.
2. Turn off lights when you are not using them.

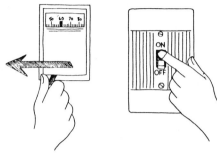

3. Keep refrigerator door closed.
4. Walk, don't ride.
5. Turn down the furnace thermostat.
6. Keep TV turned off when it is not in use.
7. In the winter keep the outside doors closed so the heat stays in the house.
8. Watch your kilowatts.

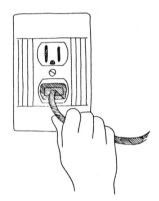

A REAL CLASS ACT: Heat Beaters

Materials: 5 glass bottles the same size, 4 boxes to put them in, 5 thermometers, some newspapers, string, a piece of woolen cloth and a piece of cotton cloth.

Moving right along:

Fill each bottle with hot water. Place the first 4 in boxes.
Wrap bottle No. 1 in a wool blanket tied to stay.
Wrap No. 2 in cotton blanket tied to stay.
Wrap No. 3 in newspapers, also tied to stay.
Pack No. 4 in crushed newspaper in a box.
Leave No. 5 out in the open air.

Measure temperature of each. Record. Wait 20 minutes and take again, then after 30 minutes.

What happened? Why do you think there was a change?

Some Energy Questions

Share questions and answers with your youngsters. In each question, decide the answer that saves the most energy, A or B.

1. Mom always does the wash in
   A -- Cold water and cold water soap
   B -- Hot water and soap

2. The washing is finished. The clothes need to dry.
   A -- Dry them on a clothesline outside
   B -- Dry them in the clothes dryer

3. At night we always
   A -- Leave the drapes open to be friendly
   B -- Close them

4. When we leave the room we
   A -- Turn off the lights
   B -- Leave them on so we won't wear out the light switch

5. We turn the dishwasher on in our house when
   A -- Every day, whether or not it is full and we want it to be clean
   B -- When the dishwasher is full

6. We open the refrigerator door
   A -- To cool us off in the summer
   B -- To take out food then close it quickly

BE ART SMART: Fancy Fading, A Shared experience

Materials: Colored paper (construction, tissue, poster paper), a sunny day, shapely objects such as a pair of scissors, a banana, some leaves, a piece of twine, a fork, a spoon and many more.

Now:

Put paper in direct sun. Arrange objects on paper with lots of space around them. Leave objects in sun from 4 to 6 hours. Remove objects and see the power of the sun.

NOTICE NATURE!

POEM
Notice Nature Through The Year
(Sing to "Freres Jacques")

In the springtime
All the world
Is giving birth
Mother earth,
Animals and flowers
Pleasant gentle showers
Mother earth
Giving birth

In the summer
When it's warmer,
Flowers fade,
They need shade
As the days grow hotter
Give them food and water
They deserve
But conserve

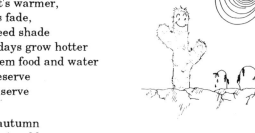

In the autumn
Weather's colder
Pumpkins grow
Sometimes snow
Gently falls around us
Like a dainty white dust
Bulbs we'll sow
Tulips grow

Winter's coldest
Nature's boldest
Trees are bare
Everywhere
Chunnukah and yuletide
Keep us on the inside,
Birds have gone,
With their song

The earth is so full of a number of things
That we should all be as happy as kings.

A CLASS ACT: Let's Make a Rainbow

Materials: A bowl of water, small mirror, sheet of white paper and a sunny day.

Let's make it:

Put mirror into bowl and let the sunshine in.
Hold up the paper so the sun, shining on the mirror reflects onto paper. Hold paper still and see the rainbow.

Encourage children to watch their world, the moon, the clouds

the weather outside
and even on TV.

23

The Moon
By Robert Louis Stevenson

The moon has a face like the clock in the hall;
She shines on thieves on the garden wall,
On streets and fields and harbour quays,
And birdies asleep in the forks of the trees.

The squalling cat and the squeaking mouse,
The howling dog by the door of the house,
The bat that lies in bed at noon,
All love to be out by the light of the moon.

A CLASS ACT: Little Sprouts

Materials: For each child, a jar half filled with water containing 2 dried lima beans. One of the beans is untreated, the other has been dipped in liquid floor wax and allowed to dry before going into the water.

What on earth will you see? Can you see which bean has been waxed?

Wait for a week and you will see that one is sprouting. The wax interfered with the natural sprouting that takes place. See how the first bean split; next, a little root appears. The shoot grows upward; the plant produces leaves and grows and grows until it is too big for the jar and needs to be planted in the garden.

A CLASS ACT: Find A Shadow

Materials: A darkened room, flashlight, paper, scissors.

To share your experiment:

Shine flashlight on walls. With a variety of objects and with your hands, see how many shadow shapes you can master.

POEM
My Shadow
By Robert Louis Stevenson

I have a little shadow that goes in and out with me,
And what can be the use of him is more than
    I can see.
He is very, very like me from the heels up to
    the head;
And I see him jump before me, when I jump
    into my bed.

A CLASS ACT: Thunder Maker

Blow up a lunch bag and hold it closed. Hit it and break it. Lightning pushes air apart and makes noisy thunder. You pushed air apart when you exploded the bag. You made thunder.

A CLASS ACT: Finger Printing

Materials: Fingers, a stamp pad, a little magnifying glass, some white paper.

Let's See:

Fingerprint some one else, not yourself. Press the round part of a finger (called "pad") on the stamp pad. Press the finger on the white paper and roll it from one side to the other. Take prints of all fingers on each hand. Give all children their own sheet of prints. Use magnifying glass to see how different all the prints are.

BE ART SMART: Spider Webbing (An Act of Nature)

Materials: A spider web that will fit on a 9" x 12" sheet of black construction paper, some talcum powder.

Let's do it!

Sprinkle powder on the paper. Gently shoo the spider away from the web. Hold paper vertically and catch the web onto the paper. Hold it up and watch it glisten.

Note: You didn't steal a spider's treasure, you took her breakfast. Some spiders eat the web every morning after spinning. *Those that don't spin, don't eat.*

State	Bird	Flower	Tree
Alabama	Yellowhammer	Camellia	Longleaf pine
Alaska	Willow ptarmigan	Forget-me-not	Sitka spruce
Arizona	Cactus wren	Saguaro cactus	Paloverde
Arkansas	Mockingbird	Apple blossom	Shortleaf pine
California	California valley quail	Golden poppy	California redwood
Colorado	Lark bunting	Rocky Mountain columbine	Colorado blue spruce
Connecticut	American robin	Mountain laurel	White oak
Delaware	Blue hen chicken	Peach blossom	American holly
Florida	Mockingbird	Orange blossom	Cabbage palmetto
Georgia	Brown thrasher	Cherokee rose	Live oak
Hawaii	Nene (Hawaiin goose)	Red hibiscus	Kukui (candlenut tree)
Idaho	Mountain bluebird	Syringa	Western white pine
Illinois	Cardinal	Violet	White oak
Indiana	Cardinal	Peony	Tulip tree
Iowa	Eastern goldfinch	Wild rose	Oak
Kansas	Western meadowlark	Sunflower	Cottonwood
Kentucky	Cardinal	Goldenrod	Coffee tree
Louisiana	Eastern brown pelican	Magnolia	Bald cypress
Maine	Chickadee	Eastern white pine cone and tassel	Eastern white pine
Maryland	Baltimore oriole	Black-eyed Susan	White oak
Massachusetts	Chickadee	Mayflower	American elm
Michigan	Robin	Apple blossom	Eastern white pine
Minnesota	Loon	Showy lady's slipper	Red pine
Mississippi	Mockingbird	Magnolia	Southern magnolia
Missouri	Bluebird	Hawthorn	Flowering dogwood
Montana	Western meadowlark	Bitterroot	Ponderosa pine
Nebraska	Western meadowlark	Goldenrod	Cottonwood
Nevada	Mountain bluebird	Sagebrush	Single-leaf pinyon
New Hampshire	Purple finch	Purple lilac	Paper birch
New Jersey	Eastern goldfinch	Purple violet	Red oak
New Mexico	Roadrunner	Yucca	Pinyon
New York	Bluebird	Rose	Sugar maple
North Carolina	Cardinal	Dogwood pine	Pine
North Dakota	Western meadowlark	Wild prairie rose	American elm
Ohio	Cardinal	Scarlet carnation	Ohio buckeye
Oklahoma	Scissor-tailed flycatcher	Mistletoe	Redbud
Oregon	Western meadowlark	Oregon grape	Douglas fir
Pennsylvania	Ruffed grouse	Mountain laurel	Eastern hemlock
Rhode Island	Rhode Island Red	Violet	Red maple
South Carolina	Carolina wren	Yellow jasmine	Palmetto
South Dakota	Ring-necked pheasant	Pasqueflower	White spruce
Tennessee	Mockingbird	Iris	Yellow poplar
Texas	Mockingbird	Bluebonnet	Pecan
Utah	Sea gull	Sego lily	Blue spruce
Vermont	Hermit thrush	Red clover	Sugar maple
Virginia	Cardinal	Flowering dogwood	---
Washington	Willow goldfinch	Coast rhododendron	Western hemlock
West Virginia	Cardinal	Great rhododendron	Sugar maple
Wisconson	Robin	Wood violet	Sugar maple
Wyoming	Western meadowlark	Indian paintbrush	Cottonwood

Book List

The Amazing Dirt Book, Paulette Bourgeois. Addison Wesley.
Animal Camouflage, Joyce Powzuk, 1990 Bradbury Press.
The Big Book of Amazing Animal Behavior, Tison and Taylor, 1987 Grosset and Dunlap.
A Child's Garden of Verses, Robert Louis Stevenson.
Cloudy, Debrah King. Philomel.
Do Not Disturb, A Book On Hibernationg Animals. The Sierra Club.
Fifty Simple Things Kids Can Do To Save the Earth, 1990 The Earth Works.
How To Hide An Octopus, Ruth Heller, 1985 Kingfisher Books.
Land Life, Hoy and Peterken. Ideal.
The Little Seashore Activity Book, Anna Pomaska, 1988 Dover.
Nature Alphabet, Jan Thronhill. Simon Shuster.
Nature Watch, Adrienne Katz. Addison Wesley.
Nicky, The Nature Detective, Leon Anderson. R. S. Books.
Nest, Barrie Watts, 1986 Silver Burdett.
101 Best Nature Games and Projects, Lillian and Godfrey Prankel, Tramercy Publishing.
Pumpkin, Pumpkin, Jeanne Tetherington. Greenwillow.
Rosy's Garden: A Child's Keepsake of Flowers, Elizabeth Lairdand. Satome, Philomel Books.
The Very Busy Spider, Erid Carle. Philomel.
Water Life, Hoy and Peterken. Ideal.
Where Butterflies Grow, Ryder. Dutton.
The Wind, Sun and Rain, Lilly and Cole. Alfred Knopf.
Young Lions, Toshi Yoshida. Philomel.

Bibliography

Birds In Their Homes, Sabra Kimball and Addison Webb, 1947   Garden City Publishing Co.
Easy To Grow Vegetables, Robert Gamnino, 1975   Harvey House, New York.
Fifty Simple Things You Can Do To Save the Earth, 1990 The Earth Works.
The First Earth Book For Kids, Linda Schwartz. The Learning Works.
How Birds Learn to Fly, Barbara Ford, 1975 Messner.
The Knowhouse Book of Experiments, Heather Amery, 1979 Osborne, London.
Let's Discover the Earth, 1981 Raintree Children's Books.
My First Nature Book: A Life Size Guide To Discovering the World Around You. Angela Wilkes, 1990
      Alfred Knopf.
My First Science Book, Angela Wilkes. Alfred Knopf.
Nature Activities for Early Childhood, Janet Nickelsburg, 1976 Addison Wesley.
Nature Walk, Susan Meredith, 1988 Art and Soul Expressions.
Nature With Children of All Ages, Edith A. Sisson, 1987 Massachusetts Audubon Society.
Sand, Sally Cartwright, 1975 Coward-McCann.
Save the Environment, An Ecology Handbook for Kids, 1974 Alfred Knof
The Seed the Squirrel Dropped, Harris and Petie, 1979 Prentice-Hall.
Snoopy's Fact and Fun Book About Sea Shores, Charles Schultz. Random House.
Treasures of the Nest, Ellen Coins and John Tveten, 1978 McKay.
Weather, Herta S. Breiter, 1978 Raintree Children's Books.
What Is a Mammal? Jenifer Day, 1978 Western Publishers.
Where's My Share? Valerie Greely, 1990 MacMillan.
Your First Pet, Carla Stevens and Lisa Weil, 1974 MacMillan.